ESTHER

FOR SUCH A TIME AS THIS

A HEROIC BLANK VERSE RETELLING OF THE
STORY OF QUEEN ESTHER

Bruce T. Forbes

BRUCE T. FORBES

To Esther and Golda—
two childhood heroines who understood
Rabbi Hillel when he asked:

If not me, then who?
If not now, then when?
If not here, then where?

PREFACE

Heroic blank verse is the writer's little-used tool for telling a long story in a metered, poetic form. Although there is no rhyming, there is a very strict metering pattern that needs to be followed, so it is still very much a challenge. It's only taken me thirty years to get brave enough to try.

Two of the greatest poets who wrote in heroic blank verse were William Shakespeare and John Milton. While Shakespeare wrote plays, Milton wrote poetry. Hence, I'm taking my artistic lead from Milton, and I hope I've done him proud. Additionally, modern writers such as Ian Doescher have given heroic blank verse a good, stiff second chance at life with his nine-volume *Shakespeare's Star Wars* series and other fantastic works. Mr. Doescher is definitely my writing hero!

The King James Version of the Holy Bible is my primary source for the story of Esther. The writings of Josephus have been used to fill in places where the Bible has unanswered questions and to add a bit of drama. I'm doing my best to tell you through the footnotes when I favor Josephus's account. The apocryphal chapters of Esther are also rich in additional information on both Esther and Mordecai.

It's believed the book of Esther was written by the prophet Nehemiah, who was a contemporary of Queen Esther, and what is now the apocryphal chapters were added at the time of the Maccabees. The Latin Vulgate and the Greek Septuagint both include these chapters as scripture, and even Josephus quotes them. As with Josephus, I will do my best to let you know when I'm following the Apocrypha.

I haven't included information concerning Esther from the Talmud. After reviewing it, it just didn't feel that it would enhance this project.

I have also taken some historical liberty in setting the stage—and to fill in blanks. This is done mostly so the reader will have an idea of the time and place and social morals and customs.

Wikipedia tell us:

> Xerxes I (c. 518–August 465 BC), commonly known as Xerxes the Great, was the fourth King of Kings of the Achaemenid Empire, ruling from 486 to 465 BC. He was the son and successor of Darius the Great (reigning 522–486 BC) and his mother was Atossa, a daughter of Cyrus the Great (r. 550–530 BC), the first Achaemenid king. Like his father, he ruled the empire at its territorial apex. He ruled from 486 BC until his assassination in 465 BC at the hands of Artabanus, the commander of the royal bodyguard.
>
> Xerxes I is notable in Western history for his failed invasion of Greece in 480 BC. His forces temporarily overran mainland Greece north of the Isthmus of Corinth until losses at Salamis and Plataea a year later reversed these gains and ended the second invasion decisively. However, Xerxes successfully crushed revolts in Egypt and Babylon…
>
> Xerxes also oversaw the completion of various construction projects at Susa and Persepolis.
>
> Xerxes is identified with…king Ahasuerus in the biblical Book of Esther.[1]

The Holy Bible tells us that the events in the book of Esther began in the second year of Xerxes's reign. History tells us that in the third year of his reign, he started a war with Greece. Legend claims this war was a cover for an operation of sending treasure caravans through Macedonia and into the Carpathian Mountains, to be hid-

---

[1] https://en.wikipedia.org/wiki/Xerxes_1.

den in a secretly constructed treasure chamber. Even though the war was a just cover, I'm sure his pride was wounded when, in the second year of the war, his army was held off by the famous three hundred Spartan warriors in the Battle of Thermopylae.

History tells us nothing concerning Queen Vashti. Josephus tells us the king continued to love her even after she was discharged as queen and sent back into the harem. So how she appears in books and movies and plays and even this poem truly is conjecture.

Hegai and *Haman* are names for which I cannot find a single correct syllable accent stress; dictionaries vary on which syllable to accent. So I've used these names while accenting whichever syllable suits the need.

I've also actively sought the thoughts and opinions of women in several forums for comments as to what Esther might have thought and felt in various places in the narrative, as my desire has been to write what a woman might have thought and felt as opposed to sounding like a man who was writing about a woman. I express my appreciation to those who replied to my requests; you did, in fact, help mold this story.

Was Mordecai an uncle or a cousin to Esther? In Hebrew the word for *uncle* and *cousin* are the same word, which simply means "male relative." The King James Bible says he was a cousin. The Latin Vulgate, the Greek Septuagint, and Josephus all say he was her uncle. Please forgive me, but I'm going with *uncle* because in my mind's eye, I see the great British actor Jim Carter playing the role.

Many Bible-reading women have created their own picture of Esther. I've encountered some who've made Esther into some sort of warrior maiden, complete with armor and chariot and Wagner's *Ride of the Valkyries* playing in the background. While this would make a very exciting music video, it's not the real Esther. She was, instead, a woman who quietly lived her religion and had the faith and courage to follow the God of Abraham, Isaac, and Jacob, even while serving as queen in a foreign dynasty. She was a woman whose faith was tested to the point of knowing she could be put to death by following God's directions and did so anyway. If she were wearing any armor, it was the [2]Whole Armor of God, which, fortunately, does *not* require a Wagner opera.

My profound thank-you to my friend—Carol A. Ray, for without her encouragement and faith, I would have stopped writing many years ago.

---

[2] Ephesians 6:10–18, New Testament.

BEFORE THE BIBLE'S RECORD BEGINS

In Susa, Xerxes' royal capitol,[3]
There stood not one, but two great palaces.
Each perched upon its own terrace, they soared
Above the city and o'er all the land.[4]
The first, of course, was for the king's own use—
And for the courtiers and counselors
Who counseled and advised and did their best
To sway the king to lead the world as they
Would have him lead. From there he ruled the world—
To India far in the east, then up
The Ni-le's flow to the Sudan[5] far in
The south, to Macedonia far in
The west, King Xerxes' word and will was law.
One hundred twenty-seven districts paid
Their homage to his name, payed taxes to
His governors, and prayed before his gods.
      But wait! One group bowed not toward thrones of men
Or gods of stone or steel. Although they did
Respect the law, and paid their tax on time,
Good Hebrew men would only bend their knees

---

3   Called *Shushan* in the Bible
4   According to archaeology, there were actually three terraces, each between fifty
    and sixty feet high and covering a total of nearly three and a half square miles.
    They literally towered over the city.
5   The rarely mentioned ancient Kushite kingdom.

And pray to their one, single, silent god—
No furnace[6] could burn hot enough to drive
Their god away; no lion's hungry mouth
Would brave the god who stood to guard those who
In faith refused to turn their hearts and minds
Away from Him and worship idols made
With man's own hands.
                              —Good Xerxes, so he did
Believe, ruled all of his known world. Or so
He thought. For in the palace of the queen,
The world revolved around *her* throne; not his.
In Persian days, when one became a queen,
Her safety and protection meant she ne'er
Stepped foot outside the palace walls again—
And so her gilded cage became the most
Extravagant of prisons ever built.
In short, her palace soon became her one
And only world; her one and only life
Became the task of making sure the king
Did visit her at night instead of the
Harīm[7]—where women ranking less than her
Did also live in splendored loneliness
But for the times their king and master did
Remember them and shared a moment of
Their time. With luck, that moment just might mean

---

[6] See the book of Daniel for the events referred to in this passage.

[7] At this point in history, it was not called by this word that we pronounce as *Harem*, but it's the word modern readers would know. This was the section of the house where women of the family lived and were protected from the world, to include the man's mother and sisters and daughters as well as his wives and concubines. Historically, it may have been part of the Queen's Palace, or it could be a separate building. Sons lived there with their mother until puberty, at which time they moved into the men's part of the house, and in the case of a royal palace, began training for both manhood and the governorship of a faraway district of the kingdom—which is why the Bible refers to governors as *princes*, as they were, for the most part, sons, cousins, brothers, or uncles of the king.

They would, at least, produce a child with him
To shower with her love.
                                  —I do not doubt
That in their lonely and secluded world
A kingly ransom found its way into
The hands of those who could supply the jewels
And silks that best would catch the kingly eye
And help his memory recall she who
Did wear it best. I do suspect the queen
Did decorate her world in such a way
That kings desired to return. Of course,
This also meant that costumes did evolve
From *Grand* to *Grander Still* in hopes his eyes
Would notice and recall and then return.
Who paid for this? No wonder kings did plot
To hide their gold and jewels in mountain caves
In faraway locations, forgetting
His best and truest fortune still did lay
Within the heart of she who once loved him
More than the riches that attended her
Far more than he who did supply them. Did
The king remove his wealth and hide it far
Away because he thought: "Enough! Enough!
I cannot see the one I love through all
The golden halls and lengthy strings of pearls?"

THE BIBLE'S STORY
NOW BEGINS

Perhaps it was to prove the riches that
Were his that Xerxes opened up the gates,
His wealth revealed to every peering eye.
One hundred eighty days—his wealth displayed,
As one by one the governors came home,
That they might be a witness to the wealth
Within the palace of their father-king.
One hundred eighty days—forgotten in
The walls of the *Harim*, their mothers hoped
Their sons might think of them; remember them;
And maybe spare a moment of their time.

[8]At this same time, a man in Babylon
Named Mordecai was woken by a dream.
"Almighty God,"[9] the man exclaimed, "what is
This dream that Thou has sent unto my mind?
I heard the noise of war that thundered 'cross
The land; I watched the earth as it did shake
And quake. I saw two dragons poised for war,
And at their cry all nations were prepared

---

[8] This event in Mordecai's life is gleaned from the Apocryphal *Additions to Esther*,
chapter 11. According to the Bible, Mordecai and Esther were living in Susa at
the opening of the story, but Josephus had them living in Babylon. I'm going
with Josephus as it makes a more dramatic story.
[9] "El Shaddai."

To fight against Thy righteous few. It was
A day of darkness, anguish, and of great
Upset upon the earth. Thy Cov'nant sons
And daughters did cry out for Thee, and from
A small and humble fountain came a flood
Of such great strength that all the darkness was
Dispelled as humble souls rode light upon
The flood, while those whose souls were weighted down
With pride did sink and drown within its depths.
    "I beg of Thee, reveal the meaning of
This dream, that I may know the role that I
Will play." The Lord, who answers prayers in His
Own time and His own way, chose to reply
When it was time for Mordecai to act.

To celebrate the end of such a huge
[10]Affair, Good Xerxes raised a tent of silks
Beside his palace grand, held up by posts
And pillars gold. There he invited those
Who represented kings and kingdoms not
Within his own control. There they did drink
At their own speed and by their own desires.
And on the seventh day the king was asked:
"The queen's own palace—does it equal thine
In beauty and in majesty?" The king,
Who loved his queen, did smile and then explain
That nothing he could build would ever be
Considered equal to the palace of
The queen, for it contained one beauty that
Could not be duplicated. "Show us, please,
This rare and wond'rous thing!" the foreign guests
Exclaimed. The king, cheeks flushed with wine and in
A state which did not always bring about
The wisest of decisions, raised and waved

---

[10] The 180-day open house.

A royal hand, and seven chamberlains
Were quickly on their way unto the queen.
    While Xerxes and his guests did eat and drink
For seven days, Queen Vashti too did sit
At feast to entertain the women of
The palace. "Dearest Queen," the chamberlains
Declared, "thy king and husband bids thee now
To come to him. He says to don thy crown
But wear no other jewels. Wrap not thyself
In silks and lace, but dress simply so all
Might see thy beauty doth exceed even
The radiance of the brightest summer sun."[11]
Queen Vashti stared in horror and alarm:
"Good sirs, I am the Queen of Persia, yes?
But more, I am a Persian woman, yes?
We are not decorations for the world
To come and gawk and awe![12] A Persian man
Doth keep us in a treasured place wherein
No man but he is gifted with our grace,
Our charm, our beauty. Please do tell the king:
If I've become as worthless as he thinks—
As worthless as the drinking cup from which
His friends do drink—then would he please retire
This wife unto a treasure house, wherein
Some stealthy thief, with skill and courage strong,
Might find in me a value that the king,
Through all his cups of wine, no longer sees."
    Between the palace of the mighty king
And palace of his queen, there lay a broad
And well-appointed boulevard,[13] lined with

---

[11] The idea that the king told her to come and show herself while nude is not supported by scripture or history. I believe he told her to come *unadorned* so his guests could see her beauty unhindered by all the decorations.

[12] A reference to the 180-day open house the king had just held.

[13] From the aerial photos of the ruins I've seen, there really wasn't much space for this boulevard, but I'm creating it as a means to showcase how the city would

The houses of the few most favored by
The king and queen. There, servants were employed
To watch the royal ebb and flow between
The royal terraces and then report.
So when the chamberlains did make their way
Unto the queen's domain, word spread from house
To house that something was afoot. I'm sure
That you can picture in your mind that as
The chamberlains returned with looks of fear
And worry on their face, word spread as if
A desert sandstorm had engulfed the town.
In anger, Xerxes stood as chamberlains
Began their tale of why the queen would not
Arrive. All entertainment died, and guests
Were wise enough to take their leave, for soon
The anger of the king would know no bounds.
As guests spilled out onto the boulevard,
Another storm of gossip spread abroad
That Vashti, queen of all the world, had dared
To disobey Xerxes—her lord; her king.
All Susa held their breath as wise old men
Were summoned to give counsel and advise.
(Perhaps he should have called wise women too?
Who might have counseled him to hold his tongue
While all good sense was weakened by his wine?)
One chamberlain, Memucan,[14] who'd been forced
To bring the queen's ill tidings to the king,
Advised the king that Vashti's words stung not
Only the king but all husbands throughout

---

have followed the gossip of the goings-on between the two palaces. I've lived in
countries with royal families, and I assure you, the public follows and discusses
their every move.

[14] Some historians believe that Memucan and Haman were the same person.
Although this would make an excellent story of intrigue, Memucan was a
chamberlain, which suggests he was a eunuch who could serve among the
women, while Haman the Adviser had ten sons—hence, he was not a eunuch.

The world. For if the queen could show such gross
Contempt unto her lord, then all the wives
In all the world would so entitled be.
But Xerxes loved his queen.[15] He did not wish
To punish her for what he'd done while in
The fickle and deceitful grasp of now
Despisèd wine.

                       —"As king, this precedent
Is yours to set—by law and by your deed.
If not, all women will take note and treat
Their lords and husbands with the same contempt
That Vashti, Queen, has grossly treated thee."

      That day, those on the boulevard did watch
As chamberlains did make their way unto
The palace of the queen, to help her move
Her privately owned things into a less
Exalted place outside the vision and
The thoughts of he who still did love the queen,
While all the things that did belong unto
The office of the queen she'd see no more.
And thus she learned to live within the world
Of silent, lonely women—the *Harîm*.
As for the king? His royal word and law
Went forth to all the world that man was meant
To rule the home, and woman to obey.

But Xerxes loved his one-time queen; he found
No joy in trying to obey his own
Decree, removing her from hearing, sight,
And touch—invisible but to his heart.
He bore not well the separated life,
Yet by his own decree[16] there was no room
Or hope for reconciliation, sweet.

---

[15] Josephus tells us that the king never stopped loving Vashti.
[16] The king's decrees could not be altered or canceled. Not even by the king.

The kingdom was in need of a new queen.
The king was sore in need of someone or
Something that would derail his thoughts away
From she with whom he never more could know
The joy and bliss of happy married life.
His friends and servants all agreed as to
A remedy. "Dear King; dear friend," they did
Advise, "Send now to each and ev'ry of
Thine governors a fresh decree: Seek out
The best of maidens, fair; with grace and charm
And beauty that might fill the empty place
Within thy royal heart…and sit upon
The queenly throne. Send with haste each maiden
To Hegai, keeper of the Women's House."
And so the search for a new queen began.
Those chosen maidens who lived closest did
Arrive almost before the Women's House
Was ready to receive them. Then came those
Whose travel took them weeks or even months,
And lastly came those maidens who did cross
The whole of Xerxes' kingdom to arrive.

In [17]Babylon, a maiden fair lived in
Her Uncle's house. Hadasseh was the niece
Of Mordecai, a leader of the Jews
In Babylon. And when her name was called,
He closed his house and joined the caravan

---

[17] The Holy Bible says that Mordecai and Esther lived in Susa and that he worked
in the palace even as this story begins. Josephus records that Esther and Mordecai
lived in Babylon and that he moved to Susa when she was chosen as queen. For
the sake of this story, I have him moving to Susa with her as she is summoned
to the Women's House in order to illustrate the devotion he showed in caring
for her. Also, translations vary between he being her cousin or her uncle. In
Hebrew, it uses the word that means "male relative." The Latin Vulgate, the
Greek Septuagint, and Josephus all say he was her uncle. I'm going with uncle as
I'm picturing English actor Jim Carter playing the role with absolute perfection.

Which bore his niece on to uncertain fates—
For he had promised to take care of her.
And when the city with its palaces
Did fill their view, old Uncle Mordecai
Did take Hadasseh's hand in his and wept.
"My father thou hast been," the maiden did
Declare. "A father's blessing give me now—
What words doth *El Shaddai*[18] put in thy lips
To send a daughter off to meet the fate
That has been laid across my path?" To which
Her kindly uncle did reply: "The God
Of Isr'el moves His playing pieces with
Such skill and subtlety that we cannot
Guess rightfully at what His moves and what
His counter moves will bring to pass. Nor doth
He take the time to patiently explain
The advantageous moves that we must make;
And so, in faith, we make those moves that best
Align us with His will."

                                        —To this, she asked:
"What is His will, that I may learn to serve
With such great faith and hope as ye have served?"
Old Mordecai allowed a smile. "Thou art
A child of Abraham; a daughter of
The law, as was your mother, and as was
Her mother. Move thy playing pieces with
The grace, the beauty, and the love that God's
Own Law has taught unto His daughters, fair.
Withhold from all until the Lord directs
The name and source of all thy learning and
Thy culture and thy faith."

                                        —The maiden gasped:

---

[18] "God Almighty" or "the Almighty God," which is how Mordecai addressed
Deity earlier in this poem.

"Deny my faith?"

                          —The old man shook his head:
"Name not thy culture or thy faith until
They see thy works and beg to know the source
Of all thy joy, that they might also walk
The path that makes of thee, e'en in thy youth,
A jewel beyond all price."

                              —Hadasseh smiled.

"If such a jewel am I, it is because
My uncle is the master jeweler—he
Whose worth is far beyond what I could hope
To ever compensate."

                          —The Old Man smiled
A happy and contented Father's smile.

"What is this maiden's name?" the guard did ask
As Mordecai and Hadasseh stepped up
Beside the gates that led into the court
That lay before the Women's House.

                              —"Her name,"
Old Mordecai began, "is Hadasseh."
   "A *Myrtle*," sighed the guard. "Do ye not know
How many maids are named for flowers and
For trees? The lass will need another name."
   "I favor *Esther*," said Old Hegai, the
Commander of the Women's House, who was
Nearby and listening. "For anyone
Can see that she is as a desert star
That guides the hopeful traveler unto
An honored, worthy, resting place, complete
With cool and calming fountains, sweet."

                              —And so,

The maiden Esther and Old Mordecai
Did share a final kiss and final hug,
And with a tear or two, they parted ways.

INSIDE THE PALACE WALLS

The Women's House[19] was now young Esther's home—
If *home* it could be called. It was, in truth,
A small community. One half of this
Community consisted of the king's
Relations: mother, sisters, daughters, all
Had each their own apartment in this large,
Secluded place, each with their retinue
Of women servants waiting for the chance
To serve their ev'ry need. (*It was into*
This portion of the house that Esther and
The other maidens found themselves assigned
A place to live while they were readied for
An interview with His Most Majesty.)
The other half of this most feminine
Community was all the wives and all
The concubines collected by the king—
Presided over by the queen. And yet,
It was in truth the king's appointed man—
Commander of the house—who ruled and reigned
This gated, closed community. The two,
I'm sure, did dance a careful, cautious dance,
Defining who was truly in control
Of any given portion of the house
And its affairs, and who was not. I'm sure
The queen did fully understand that this
Commander of the house had more access

---

[19] The biblical title for the *Harīm*.

To the king's ear than She, and so to keep
And to preserve her own authority,
She learned the diplomatic arts as she
Did smile and then cooperate with he
Who could report her ev'ry move unto
The man who was her husband and her king.[20]
        Into this world of the *Harīm* did come
Young Esther, full of hope and faith that *El
Shaddai* was in control and would reveal
His will to her. "Thou, Lord, alone are now
The only father who may light my path
And way. I do commit my heart to Thee."

        In truth, each maid, in her own way, was such
A different girl! Some cried, believing life
Was o'er. Some giggled girlishly, as if
This was a childhood game. Still others knew
The odds were not in their favor—they schemed
Of ways to change the odds, the queenly throne
Their single goal, no matter what the cost.
It was of special note to Hegai, chief
Commander of the house, that Esther's eyes
Drown not in fear-filled tears; nor did her lips
Spout giggles like a child who could not see
Beyond the day. But most of all, this man,
Who'd spent his life in governing a house
Wherein the pecking order changed from day
To day, could see no scheming on her face.
"Behold," he whispered to his guards, "a girl
Of quality. See how the natural [21]grace
That rides upon her countenance does draw
The eyes of every woman in the room!"

---

[20] Wikipedia, *Harem*, is a lengthy and enlightening article about the *Harīm* and
    how it evolved through the ages and from culture to culture.
[21] Thank you, Josephus, for this description.

"As well as ours," one brave guard did admit.
"Such grace in one so young! I'd bet my gold
She is the one who'll sit upon the throne!"
And so old Hegai showed his kindness and
His favor toward this maid from Babylon.
He found for her the best of quarters in
The Women's House; assigned the best of all
The servant girls who came from the king's house
To help prepare the chosen maidens for
Their private interview before the king.[22]

For six long months they each were bathed in baths
Of perfumes that were known to please the king.
For six long months each was massaged with oils
Of myrrh, that each would be as soft to touch
As royal hands could hope. And in that time
A maiden who arrived while thin from lack
Of food was fed until she glowed with health.
Those who were lacking in the social arts
Were trained with greatest care so that the king
Would find no fault in that regard. Throughout
This time, each maiden's hands did lose the marks
And callouses that might betray unto
The king that once she might have had to work
To help her fam'ly earn their way through Life.
        Throughout this time, Old Mordecai had found
A place to live, and daily came unto
The palace [23]gates in hopes of hearing word
Of Esther. Hegai heard of the old man
And sent a daily note that she was well.

---

[22] In modern terms, the king sent "prep teams" to get each candidate ready to meet him.

[23] Some translations refer to the gate's courtyard.

The months of cleansing and preparing came
Unto an end. And as the crowds along
The royal boulevard did part to let
The curtained palanquins pass by, a storm
Of gossip spread abroad that interviews
Had now begun. "Four hundred maidens,[24] I've
Been told," one man did whisper to his friend.
"Gods Save the King," they both agreed in their
Most rev'rent air.

                  —But what these two did fail
To understand was that each interview
Did not conclude within the curtains of
The king's most private place. He sent away
The criers and the gigglers, all—back to
The maiden's quarters of the Woman's House
(*But not to mingle with the other maids*
Who still awaited their own interview),
For they were maidens, still. The schemers did
Intrigue him, leaving him to wonder if
He could remain one step ahead of all
Their plans. Some schemers kept their maidenhood,
While others he did interview a bit
More thoroughly, only to send them off
To the apartments of the concubines,
Where all their plans and schemes would fall upon
[25]Shaashgaz, he who did command the court
of Concubines, to manage and control.

---

[24] This number is supplied by Josephus, making an average of three to four maidens per province.

[25] Sha-ash'-gaz.

ESTHER'S FAITH

The evening of the day before the maid
From Babylon was scheduled to present
Herself unto the king for his review,
Old Hegai did allow an [26]interview—
She wept upon her Uncle's lap, and with
A gentle hand he did not cease to try
To calm her troubled heart. "A daughter of
The law am I!" the girl exclaimed. "It is
Against all thou hast taught to me to stand
And willingly walk through the doors unto
The king and let him taste what is not his
To taste! Our Father Joseph fought to save
His purity from hands that had no right;
Shall I not fight for mine?"

      —"It would mean death!"
Old Mordecai did sob.

      —She took his hand:
"There is no other way that I can see!"
"Hadasseh!" Mordecai did cry aloud,
"If you could see thee as I do! For thou
Are beautiful above all maidens fair!
Thy countenance as radiant as that
Which houses it. Have faith that *El Shaddai*

---

[26] I truly doubt this sort of interview would have been allowed, but it moves my
plot along and shows how Mordecai would have raised her to have faith in and
trust the Lord.

Will open the king's eyes to beauty that
Is thine."
        —Commander Hegai, standing guard,
Insuring the proprieties were met,
Intruded on the mournful pair. "My child,
Thy Father doth not lie! Mine eyes have seen
So many maidens come and go, and I
Lie not when I do say thou art the most
Fair maiden in the Persian lands. Most fair
In body, true, but looking out through eyes
Most fair, there is a queenly spirit that
Would bring the boldest king unto his knees."
Young Esther paused and thought. "But am I fair
Enough that I may beg delay of all
His manly deeds until the wedding bed?"
Both men did nod that it was possible.
With this, Old Mordecai and Esther hugged,
And once again the two were forced to part.
     "Good sir," Hegai called out as Mordecai
Did bow to take his leave, "the prayers of all
My guards go with thy daughter, fair, for we
Have been enchanted by her smile, her eyes,
Her graceful, queenly ways. We would be blessed
And honored serving in her court." He paused.
"But thou, O Mordecai of Babylon,
Thou hast not been as truthful as thou ought!"
Old Hegai raised a hand in which he held
A necklace of great beauty and great skill.
"How is thine only brother Abihail?
The greatest silversmith in Babylon?"[27]
"Has found his final rest," Old Mordecai
Admitted warily.
                      —"Ten years ago,"

---

[27] History does not record the vocation of Esther's father, but I'm trying to build an interesting story.

Old Hegai did continue, "I was sent
"To Babylon to purchase for the Prince
A wedding gift for—"
                              "—Vashti, his young bride."
Old Mordecai broke in, the truth between
The two of them revealed. "And you did bounce
Abihail's daughter on your knee as if
She was *your* only child."
                              —"And doest thou think,"
The old commander of the house inquired,
"I could forget the beauty in her sweet
And childish smile? Her eyes that spoke such love?"
Both men did smile and nod. "From whence have thee
Obtained the once-queen's necklace in thy hand?"
The uncle asked, and Hegai did explain:
"Thy daughter, as thou proudly calls this maid,
Has made a multitude of friends among
The women housed in the *Harīm*; and one,
The owner of this work, who has withheld
Her name from Esther's hearing—*this* one has
Decreed that Esther shall adorn herself
With such a token that the king shall know
And recognize that Vashti, once his queen,
Does still advise her king, that he might make
The wisest choice that she can help him make."
He paused. "As if young Esther needs such help."
"How will she wear this thing?" the uncle asked,
"She has refused to wear a thing but what
Has been allotted equally to all!"
Old Hegai smiled wide. "The former queen
Is well-endowed with her own charms, and has
Persuaded her to don this single piece."

The morning after Esther's interview
The gossip on the boulevard proclaimed:
The curtained palanquin did not return

Unto the Women's House! It did, instead,
Pass through the gates used only by—the queen!
Old Mordecai, who'd spent the night upon
A blanket in a corner of the street
In hopes of witnessing the maid's return,
Was shaken to his senses by Hegai,
The new commander of *Queen* Esther's guards.
"It happened as we prayed and did believe!
The former queen's small token was for naught—
He noticed not the necklace 'round her neck
Until He had selected her as queen!"
"Her Virtue?" asked the slowly-waking man.
"His wedding gift to her," old Hegai did
Exclaim, "will be to keep her maidenhood
Unto her wedding day. And only when
She feels sufficiently enticed will she
Accept the blessed state of matronhood."[28]

*So Esther was taken unto king Ahasuerus into his house royal in
the tenth month, which is the month Tebeth, in the* [29]*seventh year
of his reign. And the king loved Esther above all the women, and
she obtained grace and favour in his sight more than all the virgins;
so that he set the royal crown upon her head, and made her queen
instead of Vashti. Then the king made a great feast unto all his
princes*[30] *and his servants, even Esther's feast; and he made a release*[31]
to the provinces, and gave gifts, according to the state of the king.
—Esther 2:16–18 King James Version

---

[28] Yes, that's an actual word; I did not make it up.
[29] The book of Esther begins in the third year of the reign of King Xerxes—four
years previous to her becoming the queen. That's a lot of time for these events
to be spread across.
[30] Governors and other political appointees.
[31] Proclaimed a holiday.

NO EASY ACCESS

One of the most important laws that our
Dear queen had need to know and understand
Was that her status as the queen did not
Give her unbridled access to the king.
By the decree of his Grand Sire, no one
Could come unto the king unless they had
An invitation to do so. And if
One tried to gain his [32]inner court without
An invitation, [33]guards with axes did
Stand ready to quite literally dismiss
You from mortality. The only thing
That saved you from the axe was if the king
Showed favor by extending unto you
The royal scepter. If by chance you touched
It ere the axe did find its mark, then you
Were safe. Whoa—lucky you.

                                    —And so it was

That everyone along the boulevard
Would spy the royal messenger as he
Did shuttle messages from the Queen's House
Unto His royal presence. They would note
The length of time it took the messenger
To make his way back to the queen, and then
Which royal palanquin did move in which

---

[32] Records show there was a large audience hall and a much smaller private throne
room. I'm guessing this inner court could have been that separate throne room.
[33] This is according to the writings of Josephus.

Direction. Nothing, Esther realized,
Would be spontaneous…except, of course,
When *he* would summon *her*. And *she* was wise
Enough to always be prepared to drop
What she was doing to present herself
Unto the presence of her husband-king.

    Old Mordecai could now relax. He'd seen
His brother's daughter safely through her youth;
Into about as advantageous of
A marriage he could find. True, it was not
Within the laws *Yahewah* gave unto
His Cov'nant People on Mount Sinai's slopes—
Her sons would not grow up to be sons of
The law; her daughters would be giv'n as gifts
To seal peace treaties, destined for a cell
In yet another Women's House. But this
Had been out of Old Mordecai's control!
Her name was called; she had no choice. Yet—was
Their God, with skillful touch, arranging all
The playing pieces in a pattern that
Would move His Will and Work along in such
A way that would astound and humble all?
Old Mordecai, he did not know, and so,
In faith, he thanked the Lord while begging Him
To keep his eyes upon the new, young queen.
And knowing that the best thing he could do
Was keeping track of what the king did do,
Old Mordecai did find a place to sit
And hear the gossiped news that was exchanged
Within the shade of the king's palace gates[34]—
A choice that did preserve the king's own life!

---

[34] The *courtyard* of the palace gates.

MORDECAI SAVES
THE KING'S LIFE

King Xerxes reigned for twenty years, which means
That Esther's reign was thirteen years. Of sons
And daughters we know not a thing. In fact,
There are but two short tales for me to tell!

Old Mordecai, he was content to sit
Within the shadow of King Xerxes' large
And spacious palace gates to hear the news
And gossip from the lips of those who thought
He listened not. But he was listening
As two bold chamberlains forgot to check
Before their flapping lips did fan the flames
For their own execution! Mordecai
Sent word unto the queen, that she might send
A warning to the king, that two of his
Most trusted men were planning his demise!
He even gave the names of the two men!
A swift investigation proved the truth
Of Esther's words, and just as quickly two
Of Xerxes' chamberlains were hanging in
The bright, hot desert sky, as breathless from
The view as from the pain of a slow death.
        "From whom did ye receive this timely word?"
King Xerxes asked his queen as he kissed her,
Expressing thankfulness. She then explained:

"Old Mordecai, who finds his seat beside
Thy gate to catch a word or two of just
How worthy of a husband Thou art. He
Did hear the two in all their plans and did
Send word as swift as summer storms, that I
Might send his warning unto Thee."

—"Who is
This man," King Xerxes asked, "that he believes
That he should check on me?"

—She did reply:
"The uncle who did raise me up and loved
Me as his only child."

—King Xerxes smiled
And paused before he spoke most carefully:
"Have I perchance obtained such rare and stern
Approval as a father might endow
Upon the head of such a son-in-law?"
To answer him, she smiled the smile that had
Assured her place upon the queenly throne.
The king sent orders to the scribes to set
The name of Mordecai within the scrolls
That chronicled his words and works, and then
He sent for him that he might come and live
Within the palace walls and be unto
The king an intimate and trusted friend.[35]
  [36]But Haman, trusted counc'lor to the king,
Sought ways to take revenge upon the man,
For he had caused the loss of his two best
Conspirators within the palace walls.
Appointing Mordecai an honored place
To live and to be given friendship with
The king did not set well within the mind

---

[35] The king "bid him stay in the palace, as an intimate friend of the king" (Josephus, Ant. 11.6:4).
[36] From the Apocryphal *Additions to Esther* chapter 12.

23

And heart and plans of Xerxes' newest [37]Grand
Vizier, a man whose name you have just read:
T'was Haman, bold and proud [38]Amilekite;
A people who had waged eternal war
Against all twelve of Father Jacob's tribes.
In fact, he was of royal blood of that
Now scattered race. For him to daily see
The king extend his friendship to a man
Of common blood was more than he could bear,
Because in doing so the king just might
Accept advice from this man's lips instead
Of from his grand vizier—this he would not,
Could not, allow! For now, he held his peace,
But he would find a way to separate
The King's attention from this man and put
It back upon himself, the grand vizier.

      And still the queen and Mordecai did not
Disclose their faith or culture to the king,
For *El Shaddai* still waited for the time
And place that best would serve His purposes.

---

[37] The chief councilor to the king; his prime minister. Only the king was superior
to the grand vizier in power and authority. The term was not actually used until
the Muslim Era, but it fits this situation.

[38] A-mal'-e-kit…Haman was an Agagite, the Amalekite royal family. Mordecai, a
Benjaminite, was an Israelite. Israelites and Amalekites were enemies throughout
the entire history of the Israelite nation.

HAMAN PLOTS THE DEATH
OF THE HEBREWS

It was the thirteenth year of Xerxes' reign,
When Esther had been queen for just six years,
When Haman saw his chance to take revenge
For Mordecai's offense. For six long years
Poor Haman had not noticed that when he
Walked through the royal gates, this Mordecai
Did fail to show respect! It was the king's
Command that ev'ry head would bow and show
Respect unto his grand vizier, and yet
This man, a friend unto the king, bowed not.
"How dare he!" Haman did exclaim! "What poor
Excuse has he to not obey the king?"
"Far more than once he has been asked," replied
A servant nervously. "His sole reply
Is that—*'because I am a Jew.'*"

—"A Jew!"[39]

And Haman gasped; "Hereditary foe
To all Amalekites, but more so to
An Agagite, for if the Hebrews' god
Had not defeated us in battle time
And time again, I might, e'en now, sit on
The golden throne of my own tribes! But see!

---

[39] Mordecai was of the tribe of Benjamin, but by this time, anyone who was Hebrew was called a Jew.

The Hebrews now are scattered from their lands!
Their god remains behind,[40] and in his grief
He cannot hear them when they cry and come
At last unto their aide! The gods of this
Fair land have surely smiled on me! For I
Will be the means of ending this foul plague
Of Hebrews now infesting all the world!
Dare I reveal unto the king the race
And strange beliefs of this man, Mordecai?
King Xerxes is a monarch tolerant
Of all the customs and beliefs of his
Diverse but loyal population, true—
So, I must find another charge to help
Eliminate the man and all his kind."
He paused.
           —And then he paused again.

                            —And then
He thought of how a careful twisting of
The truth served better than both truths and lies.
And so this wicked man did call upon
Those expert in the art of tossing lots
In order to discover the best day
And month that all the Persian gods would choose
For Haman's plan to then be brought to fruit.
And then he did go in unto the King:
[41]"There is a certain wicked culture," he
Began, "which is dispersed o'er all that is
Thine own dominion. They keep to themselves;
Refuse to mix their customs with those of

---

[40] The belief of many cultures of the time was that gods were tied to a geographic location—if you moved to another place you would worship the gods of that place. This is one of the reasons populations were relocated when they were subjugated—so that they had to leave their gods behind and worship their conquerors' gods.

[41] Paraphrased from the writings of Josephus—much of it was already in the correct metering.

The general populous. They look to their
Own god and won't permit the worship of
Another god. Their laws they do obey
Above the laws Thy governors decree.
They are at enmity with Thee and with
All people everywhere."

                              —And then he paused.

"If thou wilt be a benefactor to
Thy subjects, thou wilt give an order to
Destroy this most malignant group and not
Preserve a single one even as slaves
Or captives."

            —Yes, another pause.

                              —"But that

The king might not be damnified by loss
Of tribute these foul brutes do pay, I swear
From my estate some forty thousand of
My own talents, if such an act would please.
I would most willingly donate this sum
To rid thy kingdom of such misfortune."

    "I will forgive the promised payment from
Your coffers full, and give my signet ring
To thee. Whate'er thou writest in my name
And sealest with my ring shall be my word
And will."

            —So Haman called upon the scribes
Who wrote in ev'ry tongue and alphabet:
[42]"Xerxes, thy King, to all the rulers of
The hundred twenty-seven provinces...
Whereas I govern many nations, and
Obtained dominion of the richest lands...
According to mine own desire have not
Committed insolence or cruelty,

---

[42] Again paraphrased from the writings of Josephus.

But showed myself a mild and gentle King,
Ensuring Peace and Order unto those
Who show the same. Our Haman, prudent, just
Unto a fault, has come upon a most
Ill-natured nation mixed with all mankind.
Adverse to laws; not subject to their king,
Of different conduct from the rest, they do
Despise the monarchy so as to be
Pernicious[43] to our efforts and affairs.
I give the order that these men, their wives,
And children be not spared, nor shall their deaths
Be pitied, as this execution shall
Thou make upon the fourteenth day of the
Twelfth month, this present year, that when all they
With enmity toward us are then destroyed,
We may with hope obtain most peaceful lives."
⠀⠀⠀⠀As Haman's proclamation found its way
From house to house and through each marketplace,
Great shock and horror swept its way across
The city as the meaning of the words
Were fully understood. "The king we know
Would never, ever, order such a thing!"
And yet the seal he wore upon his ring
Proclaimed to all the horrifying truth
That Xerxes, king of all the world, did give
His full and absolute ascent unto
This mindless genocide. Would no one speak?
Would no one stand against the king's order?
⠀⠀⠀⠀It only takes a single one to stand,
That others might then stand with them. But who
Will be the first to stand against the might

---

[43] Injurious; destructive; deadly. He was a king known to history as being fair and
tolerant of the many religions and cultures within his kingdom, but he did draw
a line against those who were openly hostile to his reign.

Of He who ruled the world?
                               —Old Haman smiled;
He knew the plunder from the properties
Of the Deceased, claimed in the king's own name,
Would make the House of Haman...*very* rich.

ESTHER'S HORROR

[44]When Mordecai was told of what was done,
He rent his clothes, put on sackcloth, and poured
The ash of mourning on his head, and went
About the city, crying out to all:
"A nation injurious to none is now
To be destroyed!" At last he stood before
The palace of the king, but enter he
Could not in sackcloth and while bathed in ash.
    In ev'ry district where the royal words
[45]Were read, there was great mourning by the Jews—
They wept; they mourned; like Mordecai they rent
Their clothes and donned sackcloth and ashes in
Their grief and unbelief o'er the king's words.
    The first Queen Esther heard or knew was when
Her maids and chamberlains brought her the news
That Mordecai was wand'ring through the streets
In sackcloth and in ashes, praying prayers
For those about to die. "To die from what?"
Queen Esther asked in awe and wonderment.
She was exceedingly aggrieved, and sent
Some raiment out to Mordecai, to set
Aside his mourning—he received it not.
She then sent Hatach, royal chamberlain,
To Mordecai, to know what was and why.

---

[44] Taken from the writings of Josephus.
[45] Some historians believe that with the communications system of riders
   King Xerxes had established, it would have only taken three weeks for the
   proclamation to be delivered to all the far reaches of the empire.

In horror, Mordecai relayed the whole
Of Haman's plan unto the man and gave
A copy of the order that did bare
The king's own seal. He then gave charge that she
Should go unto the king and supplicate
The cause of all her people to her Lord.
Hatach reported to the queen, and did
Relay Old Mordecai's request while she
Did read the dreaded document in shock
And great alarm. "Tell Mordecai that I
Have not been summoned to the king for these
Past thirty days. He knows full well to go
Unbidden meaneth death; is that what he
Requires of me?"

              —Old Mordecai's reply
Was to the point: "Think not within thyself
That thou'll escape this holocaust because
Thou art within the palace walls. If at
This time thou dost withhold, thy father's kin
Will surely perish still. Where will the LORD
Then look to find a savior for us all?
My daughter, ever fair: who knoweth but
That thou art come unto the kingdom for
Exactly such a time as this? For just
This purpose *El Shaddai* has set thee on
A royal throne so foreign to His ways?"

    With courage few can comprehend, she sighed
And then sent word to "Gather all the Jews
And fast for me; no food or drink, [46]three days
And nights my maids and I shall also fast.
Then I will go unto the king against
His word and law. If then I die, I die.

---

[46] The Middle East custom of fasting is to fast all day and then feast at night. Queen Esther called for a complete fasting, both day and night. This was unheard of in that time and place.

[47]Old Mordecai did as his daughter begged.
The Hebrews of the city met and prayed
And fasted, no one turned away. And they
As one besought their God to not forget
His people at this time, so close to this
Unwarranted demise. Old Mordecai's
Own prayers were rich in fear that he alone
Did cause this thing by not expressing his
Respect unto Haman—"For I did not
Show [48]worship unto him, [49]nor could I bear
To pay that honor unto him which I
Do pay to Thee, O LORD, in fear that I
Would be a trespasser of Thine own laws."
     [50]Queen Esther, quite in fear of death, did turn
Unto the Lord. She laid aside her robes
Of State and covered all her fears with clothes
Of anguish and of mourning; precious oils
And perfumes rare replaced with ashes and
With dung, and then to Israel's God she prayed:

---

[47] Here we return to the writings of Josephus.

[48] Perhaps Mordecai saw the act of bowing as a form of worship and had not wanted to offend God by worshiping the wrong being.

[49] "I feared lest I should transfer the honour of my God to a man, and lest I should adore any one except my God" (Esther 13:14, Douay-Rheims 1899 American Edition).

[50] Now we jump to the Apocryphal *Additions to Esther* chapter 14.

ESTHER'S PRAYER

[51]O my Lord, thou only art our King:
help me, desolate woman, which have no helper but
    thee:
For my danger is in mine hand.

From my youth up I have heard in the tribe of my
    family
that thou, O Lord, tookest Israel from among all
    people,
and our fathers from all their predecessors,
for a perpetual inheritance,
and thou hast performed whatsoever thou didst
    promise them.
And now we have sinned before thee:
therefore hast thou given us into the hands of our
    enemies,
Because we worshipped their gods:

O Lord, thou art righteous.
Nevertheless it satisfieth them not,
that we are in bitter captivity:
but they have stricken hands with their idols,
That they will abolish the thing that thou

---

[51] I have quoted this prayer from the Apocryphal *Additions to Esther* chapter 14 without paraphrasing it into heroic verse metering. One of the things the book of Esther is criticized for is that there is no reference to God, but the Apocryphal *Additions to Esther* contains prayers by both Mordecai and Esther, assuring us that God was very alive in their minds and hearts.

with thy mouth hast ordained,
and destroy thine inheritance,
and stop the mouth of them that praise thee,
and quench the glory of thy house,
and of thine altar,
And open the mouths of the heathen to set forth
the praises of the idols,
and to magnify a fleshly king for ever.

O Lord, give not thy sceptre unto them that be
nothing,
and let them not laugh at our fall;
but turn their device upon themselves,
and make him an example,
that hath begun this against us.

Remember, O Lord,
make thyself known in time of our affliction,
and give me boldness, O King of the nations,
and Lord of all power.
Give me eloquent speech in my mouth before the
lion:
turn his heart to hate him that fighteth against us,
that there may be an end of him,
and of all that are likeminded to him:
But deliver us with thine hand,
and help me that am desolate,
and which have no other help but thee.

Thou knowest all things, O Lord;
thou knowest that I hate the [52]*glory of the*
unrighteous,

---

[52] She did not seek worldly fame.

and abhor the bed of the [53] *uncircumcised, and of all*
    the heathen.
Thou knowest my necessity: for I abhor [54] *the sign of*
    my high estate,
which is upon mine head in the days wherein [55] *I*
    shew myself,
and that I abhor it as a [56] *menstruous rag,*
and that I wear it not when I am private by myself.
And that thine handmaid hath not eaten at [57] *Aman's*
    table,
and that I have not greatly esteemed the king's feast,
nor drunk the wine of the drink offerings.
Neither had thine handmaid any joy since the day
that I was brought hither to this present,
but in thee, O Lord God of Abraham.

O thou mighty God above all, hear the voice of the
    forlorn
and deliver us out of the hands of the mischievous,
and deliver me out of my fear.

---

[53] She hated being married to one who was outside God's covenant.

[54] She abhorred wearing the crown.

[55] She evidently had times that she perhaps appeared in court.

[56] I promise I'd have reworded this into something more gently expressed had I been paraphrasing this into heroic verse.

[57] She wasn't eating at the table of Haman, the grand vizier, and in the next line she doesn't esteem her husband's feast. Undoubtedly she's eating according to the Law of Moses in her own palace. Besides the dietary issues, the Law of Moses forbids eating food dedicated to another god, and all the food from those two men's tables would have been so dedicated.

ESTHER'S COURAGE

"Deliver me out of my fear," her prayer
Did plead. Not from the situation, dire,
But from her fear, that she might do His Will.
And this, dear reader, just might be why this
Young maid from Babylon grew up to be
One of the heroes of my childhood—
Whose songs the children should sing out with pow'r!
Whose story should be shouted from the roofs,
And prayers of thanks be offered ev'ry day!
A mere two days a year are not enough
To celebrate the Maid from Babylon!
But wait, I do digress from Esther's tale…

When prayers and fasting were complete, the queen
Did put aside the ashes and sackcloth.
She bathed herself in his most favored scents,
And dressed herself in that which caught and held
His eyes and thoughts and did proclaim to all
Who saw that she was queen of all the world
And knew exactly how to dress the part.
Her crown was placed upon her head, and then
The woman, not the queen, did drape herself
With courage like a [58]mantle that would hold
Her multitude of fears and cares at bay.
How many on the royal boulevard

---

[58] A large cape such as soldiers would wear to keep their armor clean, dry, and
serviceable.

Did know that her great palanquin had not
Been summoned by the king? How many knew
The raw and pained-filled courage of the one
Who sat and shook as servants bore her toward
Her destiny? How many knew the prayers
That traveled with the queen that anxious day?
The God of Abraham and Isaac and
Of Jacob—Yes, He knew, and He did give
Her strength and courage for what lay ahead.

    [59]While weakened from both fast and fear, two maids
Assisted her in walking in unto
The king—On one she leaned most daintily
While one did come behind, lifting her train
Above the ground with just her fingertips.
And thus she came unto the king, a blush
Upon her countenance; a pleasant air
Within her ev'ry move. And yet her heart
Was anguishing in fear beyond what she
had ever known.

                —Then, having passed through all
The doors, she stood before the king, who sat
Upon his royal throne while clothed in robes
Of majesty, all glittering with gold
And precious stones—so dreadful to her view.
He lifted up his countenance that shone
With [60]fierceness and with majesty, and our
Poor Esther fell upon the maid that led
Her by the hand and fainted. Leaping from
His throne in fear, a far more milder man
Than Esther had first viewed did take her in

---

[59] The writings of Josephus and the Apocryphal *Additions to Esther* both tell the story as I am telling it for this encounter with the king. Some of it was written so perfectly in the required metering pattern that I was even able to quote several portions, much to my delight.

[60] I can only imagine that a fierce and majestic face was a job requirement, and this might have been the first time she saw his "business face."

His arms until she was herself and asked
"What is the matter? See—thou shalt not die!"
He whispered as he tenderly did lay
The royal scepter on her neck to warn
Away the axe men who were there, prepared
To carry out their dread-filled line of work.
"My Lord," Queen Esther did explain, "it is
Not easy to explain. For as I saw
Thee on thy throne—thy greatness, comeliness,
Thy terribleness…all my courage fled."
King Xerxes, greatly troubled by her words,
Did beg that she should find good cheer, and if
It was required he'd grant to her half of
His kingdom, hoping this would cheer her heart.
"I only ask that, if it pleases thee,
That thou and Haman, grand vizier, attend
A banquet in my house, [61]prepared by me,
That I may then confess the thing I ask."
King Xerxes carried her with his strong arms
And layed her in her palanquin, and gave
His word they would attend.

                    —All those along
The boulevard could only speculate
As royal healers fell in line behind
The palanquin and spent the day within
Queen Esther's gates, assuring that the queen
Would be both fit and well to greet the king
And Haman at their banquet rendezvous.

    King Xerxes ordered Haman to make haste,
That they may do as Esther did request.
So king and grand vizier did come unto
The banquet that Queen Esther had prepared.
All those along the boulevard did note

---

[61] "Prepared by me" might have been a signal that he would be eating a meal compatible to her dietary standards as set forth in the Law of Moses.

This was the first that anyone but just
The king did enter in unto the queen,
A note which elevated Haman in
The sight and thoughts of many in the town.
    The king inquired while sipping at the [62]wine,
"For what wilt thou petition? What is thy
Request? E'en to the half of my kingdom
It shall then be performed." Then Esther said
"If favor I have found within thy sight,
And if it pleases thee to grant my one
Request, I ask that both of you return
Tomorrow night for yet another meal,
Once more prepared by mine two hands alone,
And then I will obey and ask the thing
My King and Husband may fulfill for me."

---

[62] Esther 5:6 refers to a "banquet of wine." Does this mean she had invited them
    simply for drinks? Or does it mean that the wine was simply one of the courses
    of a larger banquet?

HAMAN'S VANITY

Old Haman was near bursting with delight
While making his way home that festive night.
"I am the first, but for the king, to dine
Within the sacred walls of our good queen!
A sign this has to be that ere long I
Will be within her confidence; to give
Both counsel and advice, as to the king.
The only greater thing would be for me
To find myself upon the throne I should
Have had but was denied by Israel's tribes
And their unseen, almighty god." He paused.
"But now their god is far away, and I
Am close at hand.

          —"What's this? Old Mordecai,
At this late hour, still sits within [63]the gate?
And still refuses me a bow; a nod?
To end a glor'ous night like this with such
Insult is more abuse than I should have
To bear! I cannot wait another day
To rid the kingdom of this... *Jew!*"

                    —The man
Then called his friends and wife to gather 'round
For what could possibly have turned into
An all-night whining session in which he
Reminded them of all the riches that
Were his; his multitude of sons; and ev'n

---

[63] The *courtyard* of the gate.

The honors that had been bestowed upon
Him by the king, above the honors that
The king had shown unto his own. "And I
Alone in all the world have been in to
The queen to dine! And have been asked to come
Again! No other man's been asked! And yet,"
Poor Haman whined, "It is of naught as long
As I can see that Mordecai the *Jew*
Still sits within the King's own gate!"

                      —His wife

Exclaimed: "Command thy servants to construct
A gallows [64]tall enough that all may see
The justice meted out in the King's name.
Then go unto the king and tell him of
Old Mordecai's refusal to obey
The simplest of all of the king's commands.
Thy gallows shall be high enough that from
His terrace tall the king may watch with ease
As Mordecai's dead body swings and sways."
So Haman gave commands, and servants rushed
To build a gallows tall enough the king
Could watch with ease. And then he left his house
In hopes of speaking with the king.

                      —That night

The king did lay awake; all hopes of sleep
Had vanished as he worried o'er the queen.
Of what was she concerned? What ailed her so
That she had braved her death to come to him,
A single favor then to ask? He knew
Full well that she had not risked life and limb
To ask a thing so simple as a meal;
He knew the meal was there to put him at

---

[64] In modern measurements, this gallows was built seventy-five feet into the air. The royal terraces were between fifty and sixty-five feet, so any execution by Haman could be easily viewed by both commoner and royalty, and the king could be assured that Haman was doing his job as grand vizier.

His ease, which would in turn put *her* at ease.
But why invite Haman? For this there was
No logical reply.

                 —With all sleep gone,
King Xerxes called for scribes to come and read
To him the scrolls that chronicled his words
And works. And when they read about the plot
To kill the King that Mordecai had stopped
By sending word unto the queen, he asked:
"What honor and what dignity hath been
Bestowed upon Old Mordecai for this?"

    "Thy throne has yet to give reward," a scribe
Explained.

             —"Who do I hear outside my door?"
The king did ask, as earnest voices he
could hear.

             —"The Grand Vizier, who only seeks
A moment of your time."

                —"His moments last
For half the day," the king exclaimed. "But not
Today. Pray, send him in."

              —The Grand Vizier
Entered the room while groveling so well
That he did set new records for all else
To strive to match.

            —"Of thee I need advice,"
The king appeared unto his grand vizier
To beg, which pleased the man exceedingly.
The king inquired: [65]"Because thou art in truth
My only, fastest [66]friend, I ask of thee
To tell me how to honor one that I
Do greatly love, and how to do it in

---

[65] This question is paraphrased from the writings of Josephus.
[66] And yet Josephus recorded earlier that Mordecai was given rooms in the palace
so that he and the king could be intimate friends!

A manner suitable unto my own
Magnificence." Just as you imagine,
Poor Haman was so sure the king did speak
Of him, he knew already how the king
Should honor such a man! "Bring forth the king's
Own robe and crown and his most loyal horse.
Deliver these unto the noblest man
Of all thy [67]governors to dress the man
And lead him through the city streets upon
Thy horse while shouting out to all who see
That "Thus shall it be done to any man
The king delights to honor."

                                —Xerxes smiled
And sent his servants to retrieve a robe
And crown and horse, and then he sent his grand
Vizier unto the palace gates, where he
Would then adorn Old Mordecai in robe
And crown and set him on the king's own horse
And lead him up and down each city street
While shouting out the very words that he'd
Recited to the king. And so it was
That Haman had no interview that day
That could have culminated with the queen's
Dear uncle hanging from the gallows, high.

      Returning home from what just had to be
The single most humiliating day
Of his whole life, his head covered in shame,
He barely had the time to whine before
A chamberlain did whisk him off unto
His banquet with the queen. "Old Mordecai
Will surely die," an angry Haman vowed.
"For even if I must commit the deed
In some dark, shadowed corridor where none
Can see, my hand will surely be the one
To make an end of Mordecai the Jew!"

---

[67] The titles *prince* and *governor* simply means a civil administrator.

ESTHER'S COURAGE
SAVES HER PEOPLE

In many places in the Middle East,
To sit and break the bread is to make Peace;
It means you've put aside feelings of hate,
And have begun a peaceful truce in hopes
Of better times to come. This was an act
Of [68]covenant, and one would never dare
To violate this ordinance. In this
Alone the grand vizier did so condemn
Himself, as once again he broke the bread
Within the palace of the queen. It's true
He did not know she was a Jew, but such
A lapse of simple knowledge would not save
His life when finally she did reveal
Her race, religion, and her heritage.

     The second night of dining with the queen
Began with Haman having not a clue
That it would be his last. And when the wine
Was served, the king did ask his queen to tell
At last the thing for which she wished the most,
That he may grant her wish, unto the half

---

[68] Making a *covenant* in the Old Testament included making peace treaties—a compact, a confederacy, a league—and were completed with the sharing of food—the breaking of bread. Esther may have used this breaking of bread to entrap Haman into a covenant of peace that he was breaking.

Of all he had.
                        —Queen Esther bowed herself
Unto the ground before her lord and king.
"If favor I have found within thy sight,
And if it please the king, I beg of thee
My life; I beg of thee the life of all
My people who are spread across the whole
Of ev'ry district that is subject to
Thy law and will. For we are sold, by thy
Decree, unto the Gods of Death. If we'd
Been sold for slaves, I could have held my tongue,
But through this foul decree the king is robbed
Of taxes that would leave him without means
Of maintenance or of defense! And thus
The kingdom fails, because of one man's hate."
The king was stunned; did not know what to say.
"My King, I am a Jew—by birth and by
Religion. Most of all, I am a Jew
By choice. As is my uncle Mordecai.
And now, we perish; nevermore to be
Of loyal service to the Persian throne."
        "Who wrote this foul decree and dared to put
My seal upon such evil words as this?"[69]
        The maid from Babylon stood up, and with
A sure but shaking hand she pointed and
She spoke the name: "Good Haman, who does break
The bread of friendship here within my house
And home and with my Lord, who soon will be
A widower. Because of one man's hate."
        Then Haman was afraid before the king
And queen. Poor Haman felt, for the first time,
True fear o'er what a woman had the pow'r
To do to him. She held his very life

---

[69] King Xerxes was known to seek an equity between all the races and religions
      within his empire. This discovery would have really angered him.

Within her soft and gentle hands.

                                   —In wrath
The king arose and took himself outside
Into the gardens of the queen; a train
Of chamberlains and guards rushed quickly on
To keep apace. "How could my name be used
For such a purpose as it has been used?"
The king exclaimed. "Would I destroy the Jews?
They do not worship Persia's gods, nor eat
The foods we dedicate unto our gods,
Because their god is anchored not unto
A single place, but roams the earth to where
A stalwart Hebrew man and family
Doth find a worthy place to make their home.
Destroy them? No!"

                                   —A chamberlain replied
And did rehearse the whole of Haman's plan,
Revealing Haman's heritage as well.
"My King," he did continue on, "Haman
Has built a gallows in his own courtyard,
The height of which would make it easy for
The city and both palaces to watch
With ease when Haman finally finds a way
To lift Old Mordecai unto his death."
    "It shall instead lift Haman for the world
To see," the king commanded all his guards.
    While this was going on, the grand vizier
Had thrown himself upon the mercy of
The queen, who had, by then, reclined herself
Upon her dining lounge, which means that when
The king returned he watched as Haman lay
Against the lounge as if assaulting her.
Queen Esther's panicked face became the last
Of anything poor Haman saw, as guards

Did pull a cloth across his face and dragged
Him through the boulevard and lifted him
Upon the gallows built for Mordecai.
That gave the boulevard a topic to
Discuss that day!

        —And as the body swayed
Upon the evening breeze, the king's fierce wrath
Was pacified.

        —The king remained the night
To gently, kindly show his gratitude
Unto the queen for all her bravery
And for her courage, strong. In gratitude
He gifted to his queen Old Haman's house—
His properties and treasuries; his all.
Old Mordecai was called to stand before
The king, and found himself to be the new
And quite astonished grand vizier, the king's
Own signet ring upon his nervous hand.
"A grand vizier deserves a house befit
His royal office," Esther did exclaim
As she gave unto him all that had once
Belonged unto that wicked man Haman.

    Again the queen went in unto the king
And knelt herself before his royal feet.
With honest tears she plead that all that had
Begun with Haman might be put away;
That everything he did devise would come
To naught. The king held out his scepter that
Was made of gold, and Esther rose and stood
Before the king.

        —"If it may please the king,"
She did begin, "and if I have by chance
Found favor in thy sight, and if the thing
Seems right before the king, and if I am
Still pleasing in his eyes—"

        —"Thou teasest me,"

The smiling king declared, and Esther smiled.
"What does thou ask of me?"

       —"Let it be done
To now reverse the orders Haman gave,
Ensuring death to every Hebrew in
Thy lands. For I could not endure the sight
Of all the evil and destruction that
Shall come upon me and my family!"

  King Xerxes waved, and Mordecai the grand
vizier rose from his chair. "Write now the words
That seemeth right and just, and seal them with
The king's own ring that is upon thy hand,
That no man may reverse the words that thou
Dost write."

     —The scribes were called and each did write
The order Mordecai recited to
Their ears; each in a different language that
Was spoken in the many districts in
King Xerxes' large and sprawling empire.

It came to pass that in one faraway,
Unnoticed district capitol, the scribes
Came in unto the governor with all
The morning mail. "Such news I have for you!"
One scribe exclaimed. "The Grand Vizier Haman
No longer gives advise unto the king."

  "How so?" the Governor inquired.

            —"Because
It is so difficult to make yourself
Be heard while swinging by your neck," the scribe
Explained.

     —"Who wears my father's signet ring
Today?" the governor inquired.

          —"Dost thou
Recall Old Mordecai, who always sat
Dispensing wisdom at the palace gates?

He now sits by your royal father's side."
    "Old Mordecai?" The governor almost
Did laugh. "And what great changes has he dared
To make?"
                    —"It seems," the scribe began as slow
And cautious as he could, "That Mordecai
Is of the Hebrew race. As is his niece."
    "Who is this niece that such a piece of news
Is told to me so cautiously?"
                                        —"She is,"
The scribe replied, "Esther, your father's queen."
    The governor did pause to think. And then
He thought some more. And then he thought some more.
"Just yesterday," the governor whispered,
"We were to murder all the Jews in the
Twelfth month—this very year." He paused "And now?"
    "And now thy father's seal commands that all
His governors and armies will stand with
The Jews, fighting as brothers in this fight.
You are to arm the Jews that they may prove
Once more that *Yahaveh* the Hebrew god
Stands with His followers and fights their fights
As they have faith in His almighty arm."
    "As they *become* His arm," the governor
Did add.
                    —"Your father even has decreed
The Hebrews will be free to claim as spoils
Of War the goods and properties of those
Who come against them on that chosen day."

Throughout the Persian Empire, the Jews
Had light; were glad and filled with joy. And they
Did feel the honor that the queen bestowed
Through courage few could understand. Where e'er
The king's decree was read, they held grand feasts
Of joy and gladness great. And many of

The people of the land joined with the Jews,
As Jews now stood in high regard within
The laws and policies of their great king.

NINE MONTHS LATER

Instead of fleeing for their lives, the Jews
Across the kingdom armed themselves and then
Learned how to fight. And when the chosen day
Arrived that some still thought they would have pow'r
O'er all the Jews, they found that they were wrong—
The Jews had both the pow'r and will to rule
Against their enemies. There was no one
Who could withstand, as fear replaced their strength.
The governors and soldiers all did help
The Jews—in fear of Mordecai, for he
Was great in the king's house; not to be crossed.
And thus the Jews did smite and slaughter those
Who would attempt the same of them. Across
The kingdom many fell—In Susa fell
Five hundred men who fought against the Jews.
In every other town hundreds did fall,
Including all ten sons of Haman, whose
Dark dream had been the death of all the Jews.
  Although the king decreed the Jews could claim
Their spoils of war, not one did lay their hands
Upon that which did not belong to them.[70]
  The battles raged a second day, but on
The third, when seventy-five thousand lay
So still upon the ground to which they would

---

[70] The Old Testament reader will recall that when Joshua led Israel to reclaim their
ancient homeland, the Lord commanded that there would be no spoils of war
claimed by His people.

Return, peace was restored, and such a feast
Of gratitude was held among the Jews
And those who had allied themselves with them.
   "It has in truth," Old Mordecai declared
Unto the queen, "occurred exactly as
It did occur within the dream I dreamed
So many years ago, when you were still
A maid who did believe her uncle was
The smartest, wisest man who was alive."
"My uncle *is* still such a man," the queen
Declared.
               —"Wouldst thou tell unto me this dream?"
King Xerxes asked, and Mordecai did nod:
   "I heard the noise of war that thundered 'cross
The land; I watched the earth as it did shake
And quake. I saw two dragons poised for war,
And at their cry all nations were prepared
To fight against God's righteous few. It was
A day of darkness, anguish, and of great
Upset upon the earth. His Cov'nant sons
And daughters did cry out for Him, and from
A small and humble fountain came a flood
Of such great strength that all the darkness was
Dispelled as humble souls rode light upon
The flood, while those whose souls were weighted down
With pride did sink and drown within its depth."
   King Xerxes smiled as he did take the hand
Of she whom he did love. "I do not know
Your god or all his ways, but this appears
To be a dream that all can understand.
Thou, Mordecai, and Haman, who is dead,
Were dragons, opposite—one stood for war
And one for peace. As Haman's plans did spread
Themselves across the land, it was a small
And humble fountain filled with all the faith
And courage that a woman's heart can hold

That caused the flood that drown the evil and
Did cause the humble to rise up and make
Their stand against the darkness we call Hate."

CONCLUSION

So Mordecai the grand vizier did write
In the king's name and with the king's own seal
That this last day of battle, followed by
The day of peace and rest, should both be kept
And be remembered as the day in which
The Jews did rest from all their enemies—
When sorrow turned to joy; a day to feast
And give to those who had no feast. The Jews
And all their seed throughout all time have since
Remembered well the faith and courage of
The maid from Babylon.

                    —And so when I,
A little boy so very far away from where
Queen Esther proved her faith in *El Shaddai*,
Do find myself shaking in fear and in
Alarm, I do my best to then recall
The power of a single nervous voice,
No matter how the dark may circle 'round
To try to stop that voice. And then, in faith,
I find at last my courage and my voice,
And then, like Esther, I will stand and speak.

EPILOGUE: UNANSWERED QUESTIONS

King Xerxes reigned for twenty years before he was murdered by one of his generals, which means Esther's reign was only thirteen years. Of sons and daughters, history is as silent as the grave.

What happened to Esther after her husband's death? Did she become property of the next king as was custom?

If she had sons, they would still have been young enough to be living in the *Harim* with their mother—would they have still been under her tutelage and learning about her God? What happened to them? If the next king was clearing the kingdom of Xerxes's seed, would they have been considered too young to be a threat? Or did Esther and Mordecai spirit them away to safety?

Did she even remain in the palace? Did she and Mordecai silently return to Babylon with any children she had borne? Or did they immigrate to Jerusalem, where the temple had been rebuilt?

The imaginative writer could write some incredibly inspiring but highly fictional endings to this poem (believe me, I was tempted!), but I've elected to leave you with the same questions I'm asking.

But this we know: whatever happened, she faced it with faith.

ESTHER: FOR SUCH A TIME AS THIS

A Children's Song

Bruce T. Forbes, Purim 2019

1. Esther had to make the choice of standing for the right;
   Only she could go unto the king and brave his might.
   Fearful to accept the risk, her life hung by a strand.
   Faith grew as she fasted, prayed, and chose to take a stand.

   For such a time as this like Esther I will stand.
   With courage as a mantle, while holding heaven's hand,
   The Spirit will guide onward; my fears I will dismiss.
   Like Esther I will stand for such a time as this!

2. Every day we make the choice of standing for what's right.
   Friends will laugh and call us names while we follow God's light.
   Fearful of what others think, we pause at their demands—
   Faith grows as we fast and pray and choose to take a stand.

   For such a time as this like Esther we will stand.
   With courage as a mantle, while holding heaven's hand,
   The Spirit will guide onward; our fears we will dismiss.
   With Esther we still stand for such a time as this!

Originally, verse 2 said:
"Friends will laugh and call us names and then will want to fight,"
but the women who reviewed it said that if this was about
a boy hero, then that would be acceptable, but not for a
girl hero, so I rewrote accordingly. Thank you, sisters!

Two musical versions can be found at www.
sacredsheetmusic.org/Bruce_T._Forbes.

BIBLIOGRAPHY

Holy Bible, King James Version.

Josephus. *Josephus: Complete Works*. William Whiston, trans. Grand
Rapids, Michigan: Kregel PUBL, 1960.

Apocryphal *Additions to Esther* is in the public domain and available
online at www.kingjamesbibleonline.org

ABOUT THE AUTHOR

Bruce T. Forbes is a native of Southern California, a lifelong and still-practicing Christian, and a teacher of children's church classes and leader of children's music for most of his adult life. Turning his love for writing hymns and children's songs into an even more serious form of poetry, he is now trying his hand at epic heroic blank verse to honor his scripture heroes and heroines. He and his wife raised six children while traveling the world in the US Air Force, and they are now sinking roots in Oregon's Willamette Valley, where he currently serves as the music leader of his congregation.

CPSIA information can be obtained
at www.ICGtesting.com
Printed in the USA
JSHW050041030622
26591JS00004B/108